Thursday

by Mary Lindeen • illustrated by Javier González
Content Consultant: Susan Kesselring, M.A., Literacy Educator and Preschool Director

visit us at
www.abdopublishing.com

Printed in the United States.

Text by Mary Lindeen
Illustrations by Javier González
Edited by Patricia Stockland
Interior layout and design by Becky Daum
Cover design by Becky Daum

Library of Congress Cataloging-in-Publication Data

Lindeen, Mary.
  Thursday / Mary Lindeen ; illustrated by Javier A. González ; content consultant, Susan Kesselring.
     p. cm. —— (Days of the week)
  ISBN 978-1-60270-100-7
  I. Days——Juvenile literature. I. González, Javier A., 1974- ill. II. Kesselring, Susan. III. Title.
  GR930.L566 2008
  529'.I——dc22

                              2007034079

The seven days in a week

are always the same.

Sunday, Monday, Tuesday, Wednesday,

what's the next one to name?

Did you say Thursday

was next to arrive?

You got it! You guessed it!

Thursday's day number five!

Yesterday was Wednesday.

Now that day is over.

Thursday is here.

Let's go walking with Rover!

Thursday's so busy.

There's plenty to do.

Bounce a ball, or blow bubbles.

Learn to tie your shoe!

Thursday's a good day

to get your chores done.

There's still one day left

before a weekend of fun.

A Thursday holiday

comes each November.

On this special day

we take time to remember.

We give thanks for the things

that make our lives great,

like the people we love

and the food on our plate!

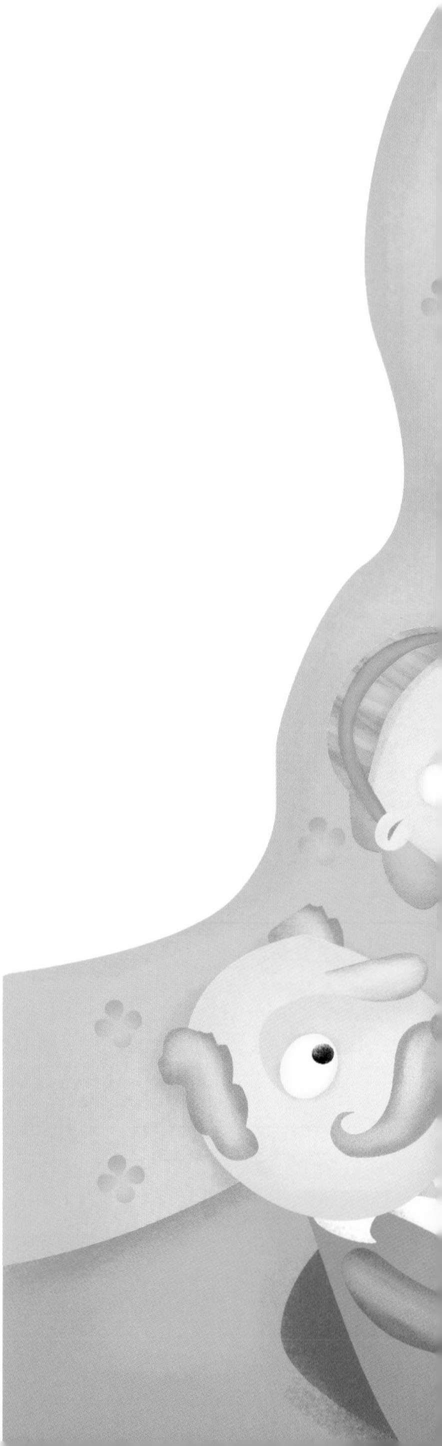

Thanksgiving Thursday brings parades and big meals,

and time for our family,

to share how we feel.

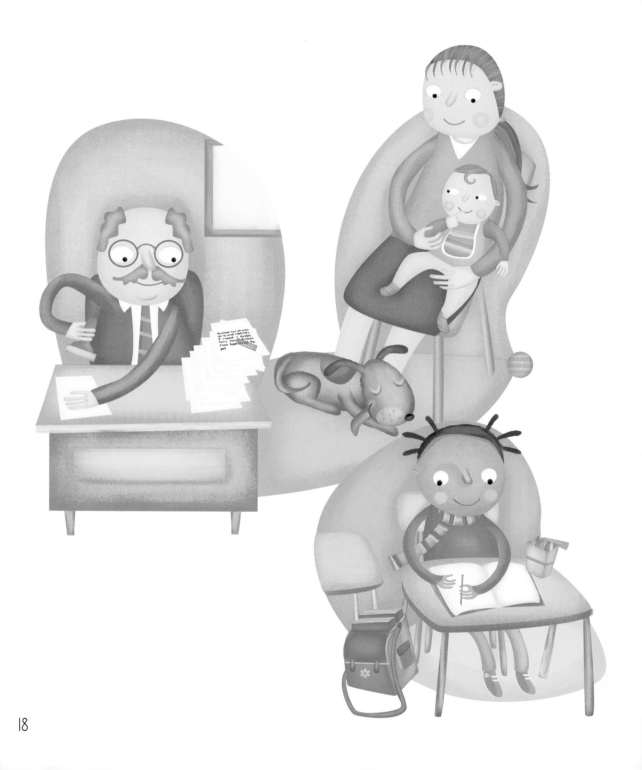

Most other Thursdays

we're at work, home, or class.

Then this fun day's over,

and it's bedtime at last.

Tomorrow is Friday.

Close your eyes for some rest.

Learning the days of the week

is the best!

The Days of the Week

1 Sunday

2 Monday

3 Tuesday

7

Saturday

5

Thursday

6

Friday

4

Wednesday

THANKFUL THURSDAY

On the next Thursday, write or draw three things that you are thankful for. Add one more thing to your list every Thursday after that. You will discover there are lots and lots of reasons to be thankful that you are you!

CELEBRATE SPACE DAY

The first Thursday in May is Space Day. Build a spaceship out of a large cardboard box, pillows and blankets, or whatever you might have around your home or school that would make a good rocket. Then get in your spaceship, and pretend that you are an astronaut blasting off into outer space!

WORDS TO KNOW

bounce: to throw an object and have it hit the ground and spring back up.

chore: the daily work of a house or farm.

weekday: any day of the week except Saturday or Sunday.

weekend: the days at the beginning and end of the week; Saturday and Sunday.

yesterday: the day before today.